HERBERT HOOVER

ENCYCLOPEDIA of PRESIDENTS

Herbert Hoover

Thirty-First President of the United States

By Susan Clinton

Consultant: Charles Abele, Ph.D.
Social Studies Instructor
Chicago Public School System

CHILDRENS PRESS ®

CHICAGO

The Hoover family: Herbert and Lou (seated); Allan (left); and Herbert, Jr., with his wife, Margaret

Library of Congress Cataloging-in-Publication Data

Clinton, Susan.
  Herbert Hoover.

  (Encyclopedia of presidents)
  Includes index.
  Summary: A biography of Herbert Hoover, mining
engineer, millionaire businessman, director of food
relief in Europe after World War I, Secretary of
Commerce, and thirty-first President of the United
States.
  1. Hoover, Herbert, 1874-1964—Juvenile literature.
2. Presidents—United States—Biography—Juvenile
literature. [1. Hoover, Herbert, 1874-1964.
2. Presidents] I. Title. II. Series.
E802.C53 1988   973.91'6'0924 [B] [92]   87-35711
ISBN 0-516-01355-6

Picture Acknowledgments

AP/Wide World Photos—16, 18, 23, 24
(2 photos), 25 (bottom), 27, 28, 37, 44, 54, 63,
65, 71, 75, 77, 81, 84, 85

Historical Pictures Service, Chicago—35

Courtesy Library of Congress—4, 48, 51, 82

National Archives/U.S. Signal Corps—38

UPI/Bettmann Newsphotos—5, 6, 9, 11, 13, 15,
17, 21, 25 (top), 31 (2 photos), 43, 45, 46, 47,
52, 57, 58, 61, 64, 66, 68, 70, 72, 76, 78, 80, 86,
89

U.S. Bureau of Printing and Engraving—2

Cover design and illustration
by Steven Gaston Dobson

Herbert Hoover campaigning in 1928

Table of Contents

Chapter 1

The Great Humanitarian

On October 18, 1914, a wealthy engineer named Herbert Hoover had an important decision to make. He had to decide whether or not to accept an unusual job offer—to feed the entire nation of Belgium throughout World War I. It wouldn't be an easy task.

By the summer of 1914, Europe was stockpiled with weapons and crisscrossed with secret alliances—agreements pledging nations to come to each other's aid in case of war. On June 28, 1914, Archduke Francis Ferdinand of Austria-Hungary was assassinated by a Serbian extremist. This one act of violence affected the whole network of international alliances. In order to live up to their promises, unwilling nations were forced to take sides in the First World War. Throughout July 1914, the world watched, stunned and horrified, as country after country was pulled into the conflict.

The Central Powers—Germany and Austria-Hungary—fought against Allied countries on two sides, Russia to the east and France to the west. To strike fast against the French, the German army swept through Belgium in August 1914 on their way into northern France. For the rest of the war, Belgium was occupied by German troops, who took over the Belgians' crops and cattle.

Great Britain, outraged by the invasion of Belgium, declared war against the Central Powers. Britain immediately used its powerful navy to blockade Germany. The blockade prevented Germany from sending out any ships, but it also kept other nations from shipping war materiel or food behind German lines. Within a short time, Belgium, which usually bought most of its food from other countries, was near starvation.

A group of American diplomats and influential Belgians began looking desperately for someone to organize a relief effort. This person had to be from a powerful neutral country, such as the United States, and had to have experience in dealing with foreign governments. The person also had to be able to understand the situation quickly, put together a huge organization, and find vast amounts of food and money. They needed someone who was dedicated, knowledgeable, persuasive, and, most of all, determined. After a brief search, the group decided that only one man fit this description—Herbert Hoover.

Before the outbreak of the war, Hoover had made a name for himself as a mining engineer. By 1914, he was running his own worldwide business, with offices in London, England; Paris, France; Petrograd, Russia; and San Francisco and New York City in the United States.

Hoover described himself and his employees as "engineering doctors to sick concerns." He traveled all over the world, reorganizing failing companies and investing in new ones—gold fields in the Klondike; oil wells in Peru; a copper, lead, and zinc mine in Russia; a silver mine in Mexico.

Herbert Hoover at the age of thirty-four

Hoover had become a millionaire several times over. With the coming of war and the demand for ores and metals, he stood to make a huge profit. On the other hand, if he took up the relief of Belgium, he would have to give up his business for a while. He asked for a day to make up his mind.

Now that he had achieved such success, Hoover was becoming interested in some kind of public service. The feeding of Belgium was work on the large scale he enjoyed. It was also a task worthy of all his energy, fervor, and expertise. He called it "the greatest job Americans have undertaken in the cause of humanity." To a close friend he confided, "Let the fortune go to hell."

Hoover accepted the challenge on two conditions. First, he was to have "absolute command" over the whole organization; and second, he was to serve without pay. As Hoover explained, "I could not appeal to others to sacrifice without sacrifice myself." The committee agreed that Hoover needed authority. He would have to manage huge sums of money and work with warring governments as well as purchase, ship, and distribute tons of food from all over the world.

Once he accepted, Hoover had to act quickly. Major Belgian cities were down to less than a week's supply of bread. He immediately gathered a group of Belgians and American diplomats and engineers to form the Commission for Relief in Belgium, known as the CRB. Then he called Chicago markets and ordered ten million bushels of wheat before the price went up. He trusted that Belgian money and charitable contributions would pay for the food. As months went by, however, the CRB found itself with only $6 million to spend and with food orders totaling over $30 million on the way.

Hoover had to seek help from England and France. Before the Allies would contribute, they insisted that Germany stop taking food and cattle from the Belgians. Otherwise they said, sending Belgium food would be like feeding the German army. Hoover himself made the dangerous trip to Berlin and got the Germans to agree. With this agreement in hand, Hoover returned to appeal to the British cabinet. They agreed to contribute approximately $5 million a month to the CRB. For the moment, the relief effort could continue.

Motor convoy on the way to Verdun, France, in 1916

As the war went on, the cost of feeding Belgium rose to $25 million a month. Hoover kept on in his blunt way, twisting arms and raising money. British Prime Minister Herbert Asquith once said to Hoover, "You told me you were no diplomat, but I think you are an excellent one, only your methods are not diplomatic."

Hoover was a powerful but not a particularly charming figure. At age forty, his broad forehead, firm-set mouth, and square face gave the impression of dogged determination. In spite of his world travels, Hoover had never developed any social ease or grace. When he had something to say, he came straight to the point, often reciting facts while he paced back and forth jingling the change in his pocket. He usually wore conservative blue suits and stiff collars, but he didn't notice when his suit looked rumpled or his shoes looked scuffed.

In every way, Hoover made it plain that he wanted action, not chatter. By the end of the war, he had coaxed $109 million from Great Britain, nearly $205 million from France, and $386 million from the United States for the CRB.

Hoover knew how to give his arguments force. First, he used public opinion. Neither of the warring sides wanted to be responsible for starving a whole nation. Hoover made sure that the world knew about Belgium's plight and that leaders on both sides knew about the world's sympathy and outrage. As a result, he got what he needed for the CRB, whether it was money to buy food or passports to let his men move freely in and out of warring countries. Hoover's own passport from Germany read, "This man is not to be stopped anywhere under any circumstances."

Besides using public opinion, Hoover also brought to bear his own incredible memory and command of facts. While telling pathetic and stirring stories was never his way, he could tell government leaders just how many people were starving and how much food it would take to feed them. He had information on which countries had surplus food, how much it would cost to obtain it, and how many ships it would take to get it to Belgium. For every Belgian community, the CRB knew which people could afford to pay for their food and which ones could not. Hoover could explain exactly how the CRB's money would be spent, and he could promise that the money wouldn't be wasted. By the end of the war, the CRB had spent a billion dollars, but the cost of running the organization itself amounted to less than one-half of one percent of that total.

Herbert Hoover, as Food Administrator, in Paris in 1917

Once he had the money, Hoover had to decide what foods to buy. The CRB needed to provide a well-balanced diet at the lowest possible cost. For example, to give the people some protein, the CRB sent beans (102,000 tons) instead of meat because beans were much cheaper and would not spoil easily.

Hoover had experts on nutrition help set a goal of 1,800 calories a day for each adult. Children needed more, so the CRB invented and manufactured their own enriched crackers.

At noon every day, 2,500,000 children received an extra meal of stew, milk, and CRB crackers. As Hoover described it:

"The troops of healthy cheerful chattering youngsters lining up for their portions . . . were a gladdening lift from the drab life of an imprisoned people. And they did become healthy."

In some instances, however, Hoover had to persuade the people to accept the foods he obtained. When the CRB sent in cornmeal as a substitute for wheat flour, the Belgians at first refused to eat it. They thought it was fit only for animals.

Hoover took over an ice-skating rink in Brussels and arranged corn bread cooking lessons for hundreds of Belgian housewives. Corn bread caught on; even after the war ended, Belgians continued baking it.

To keep world support, the CRB had to be careful that none of their food went to the Germans. They gave the Belgians rationing cards and even special money to exchange for food.

In one case, a serious problem arose when British soldiers reported that the Germans were making grenades from empty CRB condensed milk cans and building their trenches with sandbags made from CRB flour sacks. From that point on, the people had to return every empty sack and can to the CRB.

A British cargo of wheat and rice being sent to Belgium in 1914

German submarines made it difficult and dangerous to get supplies to Belgium. In spite of their CRB flags and a huge sign "Belgian Relief Commission" stretching the length of the boats, more than a dozen CRB ships were sunk in 1917. Some were torpedoed by German submarines; others were blown up by underwater mines. Food deliveries dwindled until neutral Holland and Spain persuaded the Germans to let CRB ships through.

The first American troops to land on French soil, parading in St. Nazaire

German submarine attacks on U.S. ships brought the United States into the war on the Allies' side on April 6, 1917. Hoover's work for the CRB convinced President Woodrow Wilson and the American people that he was just the man to manage America's wartime food supply. He was known as the Great Humanitarian. With his moral energy, breadth of understanding, and engineering efficiency, Hoover seemed cut out to be a national leader. As years went by, popular admiration for Hoover grew until he was elected president by an overwhelming majority in

Hoover supervising a food shipment to Europe

1928. Four years later, in 1933, Hoover lost his bid for a second term by an even greater margin. He left office the most unpopular president in American history.

Hoover's work for the CRB stands as a great and humane achievement. Late in his life, however, Hoover called it "the worst mistake of my life." He wasn't sorry about the results of the Belgian relief—his work had helped keep millions of people from starving to death. He meant that without the nationwide recognition and admiration he had won as head of the CRB, he never would have been elected president.

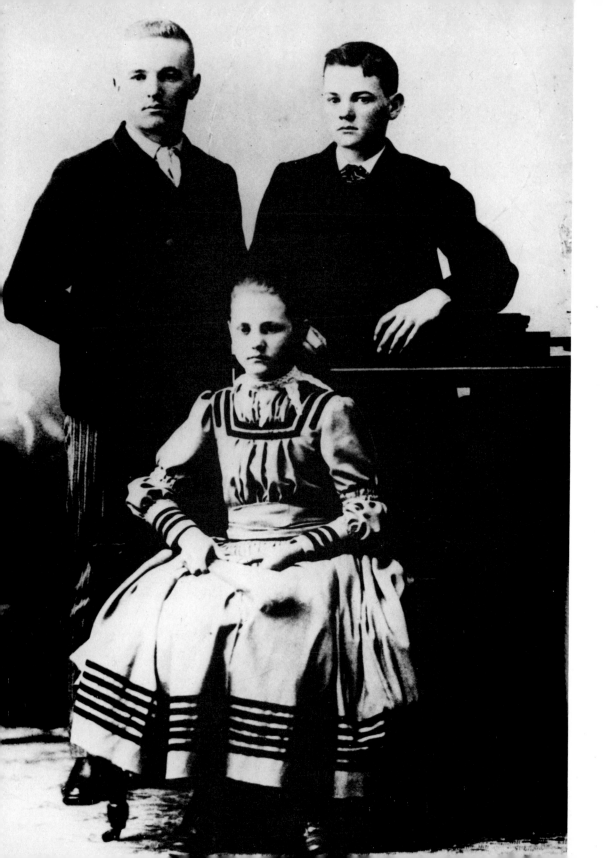

Chapter 2

From Quaker Orphan to Progressive Engineer

In his *Memoirs*, Herbert Hoover wrote about the great sledding hill and swimming hole in his birthplace, West Branch, Iowa. In the 1870s, West Branch was a small, austere farming town with brown frame houses, a plain Quaker meetinghouse, a newspaper office (run by one of the few Democrats in town), and a blacksmith shop run by Hoover's father, Jesse. Everyone depended on horses to pull their plows and buggies. Jesse Hoover did a good business shoeing horses and selling plows, wagons, cultivators, and barbed wire. He and his wife, Hulda, had three children: the oldest, Theodore, called Tad, was born in 1871; then came Herbert—Bert to his family—born August 10, 1874; and finally, May, born in 1876.

The unpaved roads of West Branch turned to mud every spring and after summer rains. One wet summer, the mud was so deep that little Bert kept getting stuck. His father plucked him out time after time, until he began calling Bert his "little stick in the mud." As the Hoover children grew up, they did chores such as hoeing, weeding, or picking potato bugs—one penny per hundred bugs.

On Sundays, the entire family went to the Quaker meetinghouse, where Bert remembered sitting for hours in the quiet church. At a Quaker meeting there are no ministers or rituals. Quakers believe that God fills each individual with an inner light. The people sit silently, waiting to feel the presence of God in themselves. Anyone who feels inspired may speak out. The Quaker belief in the equality of the sexes was obvious in the West Branch services. Bert's mother, Hulda, frequently spoke at meetings, and his great-grandmother, called Aunt Rebecca, was one of the elders of the church.

In keeping with the Quaker belief in simplicity, the West Branch meetinghouse was very plain and unheated, although in summer screens were put up to keep out the horseflies. Hoover wrote about Quaker meetings: "All this may not have been recreation, but it was strong training in patience."

Bert gained much more than patience from his Quaker upbringing. A strong sense of responsibility to the community and a belief in the worth of the individual stayed with him his entire life. Hoover's willingness to tackle the huge humanitarian task of feeding Belgium during World War I seems a natural outgrowth of his Quaker upbringing. So does the fact that he accomplished this great task in a hardheaded, thrifty, and efficient way. Quakers didn't expect to find happiness only in the next world. With hard work and thrift, they believed that people could build a prosperous and orderly world right now. The Hoover family was a good example. Jesse's business prospered, and after a time he moved the family to a larger house.

Herbert's parents, Hulda and Jesse Hoover

Then in 1880, tragedy struck—Jesse Hoover died of heart trouble. Left with three children to support, Hulda took in sewing and tried to stretch her small income as far as she could. She also became more active as a speaker at revival meetings throughout Iowa. After one meeting in a neighboring town, she walked home through a snowstorm. Her cold turned into pneumonia, and the Hoover family suffered yet another blow. Hulda died in February 1884. The three orphans were separated and sent to live with different relatives.

Now nine years old, Bert Hoover was already a bashful little boy. But with his mother's death, Bert lost his home and his entire family. His bashfulness turned into a permanent reserve. All his life, Hoover would seem cold and unconcerned to many people. His public speeches would be criticized as a collection of facts without feelings. Whatever his feelings were, the orphan boy who later became the Great Humanitarian learned to keep them to himself.

When he was eleven, Bert traveled seven days by train to Oregon, where he was to live with his uncle, Dr. Henry John Minthorn. Minthorn was a stern and enterprising man who believed in hard work. He kept young Hoover busy tending his horses, splitting logs for the stove, and helping to clear a forest of fir trees. He used to take Bert along as he drove his horse and buggy around the rough country roads visiting his patients.

When Minthorn started a real estate business in Salem, Oregon, Bert left high school to work in the office for a salary of $30 a month. He seemed to have a knack for business, and in a short time he knew every detail of the firm's affairs. Talking with an engineer in the office started Hoover thinking about a career in engineering.

His uncle always assumed that Herbert would attend a Quaker college. He was unpleasantly surprised to find that his nephew had plans of his own to attend a brand new university called Stanford in California. After a summer of special tutoring (Hoover had failed all of the entrance exams except math), Hoover was accepted into Stanford's first class.

Herbert (seated, left) with his Stanford University surveying squad

On his train ride to Oregon back in 1885, the eleven-year-old Hoover had been disappointed to see that the fabulous Rocky Mountains were made only of dirt and rocks. By the time he entered college, he had gotten over his initial disappointment. He decided to study geology with the idea of becoming a mining engineer. Hoover immersed himself in his field. He studied geology with Professor John Caspar Branner, worked part time typing in the Geology Department to pay for his room and board, and got summer jobs tracing rock formations for geological surveys.

Above: A reconstructed version of Hoover's West Branch, Iowa, birthplace
Below: Herbert (left) at the age of five, with his brother, Theodore

Above: At Pacific College, Newberg, Oregon, Herbert is shown second from the
left in the front row. At left is his uncle, Dr. John Minthorn.   Below: Hoover
(back row in coat) as team treasurer of the Stanford football team

Years of living with various relatives and working long hours hadn't given Hoover much social confidence. Nor had he developed much skill in speaking or writing. In fact, Hoover barely passed his college writing courses. At college he remained a shy, blunt young man, striding across campus with his hands in his pockets and his eyes on the ground, but he did make a few good friends. One of them, Will Irwin, wrote about Hoover:

"Affection for Hoover [was] not a sudden dazzling discovery but a gradual dawning. The crown of his personality was his shyness."

Among the people he met was the warm, athletic, adventurous Lou Henry, the only woman in the Geology Department. By the time he graduated, Lou and Bert had reached an understanding—they would marry as soon as he could afford to support a family.

Hoover graduated from Stanford in 1895 with $40 to his name and a degree in geology. The country was in the middle of a depression—a period of low economic activity when there is a shortage of both money and jobs. Young Hoover was not at all worried about the state of the economy: "I had never heard of depressions. No one told me that there was one afoot. So I did not need to worry about that. Nor did I have to worry about what the government was going to do about it."

Hoover found a job, pushing a car deep in the tunnels of a California mine. For every ten-hour night shift, Hoover earned two dollars. When work at the mine slowed down, Hoover had to go looking for another job. He was hired as a typist for a San Francisco engineering firm. The head of

Hoover as a young engineer in Australia

the firm, Louis Janin, promoted Hoover to engineering
jobs and, two years later, recommended him for a job with
an English mining firm, Bewick, Moreing and Company.

Bewick, Moreing wanted an experienced mining engineer to run their Australian gold mines. Hoover was only
twenty-three years old, with less than two years' engineering experience; however, Janin encouraged him to take
the job. Hoover grew a mustache to help him look older,
bought some tweeds for his appearance in England (he
never actually wore them), and took the job.

Chapter 3

The Great Engineer

Bewick, Moreing sent Hoover by steamship to Australia and then by train five hundred miles inland to a blistering hot, dusty mining settlement called Coolgardie. The buildings were made of corrugated iron; there weren't any trees, just low bushes. To vary his diet of toast, cocoa, and canned sardines, Hoover once tried to grow a garden, but only two cabbages survived. Growing them used up $500 worth of water.

With only an inch of rainfall a year, Coolgardie didn't have enough water for keeping horses or for using older mining techniques. Hoover rode camels instead of horses and helped introduce the filter press, which caught the water used in mining processes so that it could be reused.

A camel, according to Hoover, "is even a less successful creation than a horse. . . . No amount of petting will inspire him with affection. His long neck enables him to bite one's leg unless he is constantly watched." Hoover formed these opinions after riding camels on his many trips to scout new prospects, or partially developed mines. A prospect called the Sons of Gwalia mine looked especially promising to Hoover. His report led Bewick, Moreing to buy it for $500,000, and over the years the mine produced $55 million in gold.

Opposite page: Hoover in 1900

Bewick, Moreing next asked Hoover to manage their mines in China. Hoover accepted. Since he had received a hefty raise, he sent a cable to his former classmate, Lou Henry; it read, "Will you marry me?" Hoover sailed back to California and married Lou on February 10, 1899. The couple, with plenty of books for their new home, got back on a steamship for China. Once on the mainland, Lou set up their first house in Tientsin.

Hoover was to start up a modern coal mine and build a port for shipping the coal. When he accepted the job, the Chinese emperor Kuang-hsu was eager for Western help in developing his country's mines and other resources. As Hoover observed, many Western developers were eager to make as large a profit as they could on Chinese resources while sharing as little of it as they could with the Chinese. Hoover suggested a mining law to keep the Chinese mines under better government control, but by then the young emperor was in prison and the whole country was turning against grasping Westerners.

In 1900, an angry group of Chinese called the Boxers was rising up. (Their name in Chinese was I Ho Tuan, meaning "righteous harmonious fists.") The Boxers decided to wipe out every trace of Western influence in China. This included the telegraph lines, the railroads, the mines, the missions, and the Westerners themselves.

The Hoovers were trapped with other foreigners in Tientsin. The Chinese troops brought in to protect the settlement turned on it and began bombarding it from the Chinese section of the city. Shelling and rifle fire went on for thirty long days.

Above: The Boxer Rebellion, China, 1900
Below: Foreign troops sent to help quell the Boxer Rebellion

Hoover helped take bags of rice and sugar and peanuts out of warehouses and pile them up to barricade the streets. Lou Hoover worked in the makeshift hospital, nursing the wounded. The Hoovers got around by bicycling close to the barricades to avoid the bullets, although one day a bullet punctured Lou's bicycle tire. After a month, they were rescued by army troops who finally put down the Boxers. Hoover immediately sent a cable to Lou's father in California. It contained one word: "Safe."

After the Boxer Rebellion, the Chinese gave Bewick, Moreing more authority over a greater area than the company had enjoyed before. Hoover became the manager of a huge coal mining enterprise. His job now was to repair the damage done to rail lines and equipment during the rebellion, then turn money-losing mines into profitable ones. Even though Hoover accomplished this task in short order, he no longer had a free hand in managing the mines after the fall of 1901.

Belgians had bought control of the mines from Bewick, Moreing and sent their own director, Emile Franqui, to oversee operations. Franqui and Hoover could not get along. They disagreed on how much control the Chinese should have in running the mine. Hoover had signed an agreement giving the Chinese an equal voice with the foreigners, and Franqui wanted to cancel the agreement. Frustrated and angry, Hoover left China.

Back in England he was made a partner in Bewick, Moreing; this meant that, instead of simply working for the company, he became a part owner. At twenty-seven years of age, Hoover was young to be a partner. Instead of working in the office, he chose to travel all over the world, visiting the company's mines and searching for new ones.

In 1905, he traveled to Burma to look at an ancient silver mine. He and his guide entered the old tunnel and found rich deposits of silver. They also found that they were following fresh tiger tracks into the tunnel! The two men exited the mine in great haste. Later, Hoover was able to convince his company to open the old site. Although it took years to hit the big deposits, this silver mine fulfilled Hoover's expectations and, in the process, made him wealthy.

The Hoovers' first son, Herbert, Jr., had been born in 1903. When the baby was five weeks old, the Hoovers took him along to Australia, carrying him in a basket. Their second son, Allan, was born in 1907, and he too began traveling as an infant. It was hard to keep up with Hoover—his work for Bewick, Moreing took him around the world five times in five years.

By 1908, Hoover found he could not agree on much of anything with his business partner, Charles Moreing, so Hoover sold his share of Bewick, Moreing and started his own business. When he left Bewick, Moreing, he figured he was earning one of the "largest engineering salaries of the period." Within two years of starting his own business, he was earning even more. He reorganized failing companies, hunted for new mining prospects, and found investors to pay for developing the best ones. By now he was used to dealing with large enterprises and equally large amounts of money. Among engineers and investors, he was known as the Great Engineer.

Wherever Hoover went, he brought in American engineers and modern American methods and machinery. In Australia, he was called "Hail Columbia" Hoover because of his preference for his own countrymen.

The longer Hoover worked in foreign countries, the more he wanted to come home to the United States to live and work. The more he saw of other societies—the masses of poor people in China, for instance, and the privileged aristocrats in England—the stronger was his faith in American democracy. In his native country, each individual had a chance to use his or her talents, regardless of birth or rank.

Hoover had very personal reasons for believing in the values of the democratic system. He saw his own rise from poor orphan to millionaire as an American success story. In his eyes, democracy was not just high-minded but sensible and efficient. It was only natural that the most efficient use of talented people should bring about the most prosperous and advanced society.

In those years, American society was indeed prosperous and advancing by leaps and bounds. However, the tremendous growth of industry was raising equally troublesome questions for Americans. In many cases, the founders and owners of big industries—steel, automotive, and telephone and telegraph—were amassing huge fortunes, paying low wages to their workers, and creating monopolies. Monopolies were giant businesses that could eliminate any competitors and then charge high prices and pay low wages as they pleased. How much control should the government have over these monopolies?

Hoover in Paris when he was Food Administrator

The question had no easy answer. Some people, known as Socialists, believed that government should take over the major industries and run them to make sure that workers got paid a fair share of the profits. Others, called *laissez-faire* ("let it be") conservatives, believed that government should stay out of business altogether. They felt that interfering with business would be interfering with individual liberties.

A third group, called progressives, tried to take a middle path. They believed that the government should encourage responsible cooperation between workers and owners while making laws to prevent abuses like monopolies. Monopolies threatened democratic principles because they put an end to competition, thus denying people an equal opportunity to succeed. Progressives believed that government should guarantee people an equal opportunity to compete and prosper. This principle seemed only logical. After all, industry couldn't prosper unless millions of workers could afford such things as going to the movies, riding airplanes, and buying cars, vacuum cleaners, radios, refrigerators, and other goods.

Hoover was a progressive. What society needed, in Hoover's opinion, was some scientific management. He believed that no one was better suited to help America adjust to its new industrial power and wealth than an engineer. Hoover felt confident that social problems could be solved the same way mining problems were solved—by relying not on tradition but on facts and logic. Hoover described the engineer as "an economic and social force. Every time he discovers a new application of science, thereby creating a new industry, providing new jobs, adding to the standards of living, he also disturbs everything that is. . . . He is also the person who really corrects monopolies and redistributes national wealth."

Later on, in 1922, the ideas from his Quaker upbringing, his engineering training, and his world experience all came together in *American Individualism*, a book Hoover wrote about the American system. In 1914, Hoover was

The first convoy of American troops arrives in France, June 1917

looking for a chance to act on his beliefs in some kind of
public service. The plight of Belgium in World War I gave
him the opportunity. Hoover put other men in charge of
his mining business and gave all his time to Belgian relief
from 1914 until 1917, when the United States entered the
war. Then in May 1917, President Woodrow Wilson asked
Hoover to come to Washington, D.C., to serve as his wartime Food Administrator.

Chapter 4

Food Dictator

Once again, Hoover insisted on two conditions before taking up the job of Food Administrator. First, he wanted the authority to make decisions without consulting any board or commission. Second, he wanted to serve as a volunteer, without any salary. Some people were worried about giving so much power to one man. Newspaper headlines called Hoover "Food Czar" and "Food Dictator." After all, the Food Administrator would control the entire country's food supply, as Hoover put it, "from the soil to the stomach."

He controlled what farmers produced; how much they were paid for their products; how much and what went to the American army abroad, to their European allies, and to grocery stores at home; and how much the grocery stores could charge their customers. This one man, who had never been elected to office, had almost total authority over farms, food shippers, processors, manufacturers, stores, and ultimately, homes.

Early in the war, Hoover and Wilson had watched the European Allies waste time on political squabbling and disorganization. By 1917, it was clear that the Allies could no longer afford to waste time, food, or human lives; the pressures of war called for a strong, efficient organization. British and French ships would be needed to help carry the American army, with all its supplies and equipment, across the ocean to Europe. Warships had to sail along with transport ships to protect them from German submarines. As a result, the British and French would not have enough ships to bring in food—they would have to rely on the United States for their food supply. In spite of two bad harvests in a row, the U.S. would have to find enough food to feed itself and its European allies. To accomplish this enormous task, Hoover persuaded Wilson that a single authority was necessary.

Hoover's work with the CRB had convinced everyone that he would not abuse his tremendous power. Hoover, the progressive engineer, did not plan to act like a dictator but to rely on the voluntary cooperation of the American people. The people's job was to conserve food. Housewives were urged to serve their families fish instead of meat and vegetables instead of wheat. Hoover used advertising to gain people's cooperation. He had messages like "Food Will Win the War" spread in newspapers, posters, magazines, billboards, and even movies. One campaign urged people to clean up their plates. Another slogan went, "When in doubt, serve potatoes."

Hoover's policy worked. Households all over the country pledged to follow the Food Administration's rules and displayed Food Administration window stickers. "Hoover-ize" came to mean saving for a worthy goal. One Valentine's Day card read, "I can Hooverize on dinners, and on lights and fuel, too, but I'll never learn to Hooverize when it comes to loving you!"

Daily conservation of food in millions of homes meant that more food was available to send overseas. More importantly, it meant that Americans could and would make sacrifices for the common good without being forced to do so by government rationing.

Besides convincing the American people to conserve food, the Food Administration also had to persuade farmers to produce more while keeping food dealers from charging more.

For example, because of poor harvests, wheat was in short supply. If food dealers were allowed to compete for the supply, the price of wheat would have risen dramatically. Instead, a Fair Price Committee set a fixed price of $2.20 per bushel for the grain—a price that covered the cost of growing it and gave the farmer a profit. Once farmers could be certain of a fair return for their crops, they planted more and more fields in wheat.

President Wilson made Hoover chairman of the Grain Corporation, a government agency that bought up huge quantities of wheat, always at the fixed price, when supplies were plentiful. The Grain Corporation stored the surplus wheat and released it for sale when the supply was low. In this way they kept the price and the supply steady. It prevented people from hoarding for fear of shortages or out of the desire to make a huge profit later.

All of these measures kept food streaming over to Europe. By Hoover's own reckoning, the amount of exported wheat and other breadstuffs tripled from 3,720,000 tons per year before the war to a peak of 11,762,000 tons in 1918!

On November 11, 1918, Germany signed an armistice, agreeing to end the fighting. World War I was over, but Europe's need for food was as pressing as before. The war had left the European nations impoverished, disorganized, and without food to last out the winter. President Wilson asked Hoover to come with him to Paris and organize the relief of Europe.

Hoover and Wilson firmly opposed using food as a political weapon, but the victorious Allies kept up the food blockade against Germany even though the war was over. They were determined to make Germany suffer for its part in the war. One British admiral remarked to Hoover, "Young man, I don't understand why you Americans want to feed these Germans." In his blunt way, Hoover replied, "Old man, I don't understand why you British want to starve women and children after they are licked." The food blockade was finally lifted in March 1919.

Lifting the blockade was only the first of many struggles that President Wilson faced during the treaty-making process. Wilson had hoped for what he called a peace without victory, meaning a treaty that would not take revenge on Germany and Austria for the war. Hoover had seen hatred and desire for revenge growing throughout the war, and he did not have high hopes for Wilson's idealistic peace terms. In the end, the Treaty of Versailles ignored

World leaders meet in 1918 to discuss the Versailles peace treaty. Left to
right are: Vittorio Orlando of Italy, David Lloyd George of England,
Georges Clemenceau of France, and Woodrow Wilson of the United States.

most of Wilson's suggestions. Among other things, the
treaty forced the defeated nations to give up territory and
pay the victor nations heavy reparations, or payments to
make up for war damages.

Hoover stayed in Europe for almost a year, reorganizing
railroads and canal shipping, finding and purchasing food,
and moving it where it was needed. All over Europe, in
both victorious and defeated nations, there were thousands
of orphaned and starving children, whom Hoover made
special effort to feed and clothe.

Food Administrator Hoover with Pope Pius XI in 1919

On a visit to Warsaw, Poland, Hoover was honored by a parade of 50,000 of the children he had helped to feed. Singing "The Star-Spangled Banner" over and over again, the children marched past Hoover from noon until dark. After watching this display of gratitude for a while, a French general told Hoover, "There has never been a review of honor in all history which I would prefer for myself to that which has been given you today." Hoover himself was touched by the children's parade; however, he still remained a firmly unsentimental figure. "While the inspiration to reform comes from the human heart,"

President Wilson and Belgian King Albert view a battlefield in Belgium, 1919.

Hoover said, "it is achieved only by the intellect." He was interested in facts, not sob stories; in getting the job done, not in getting decorations. (He accepted only two awards for his relief work — the French Legion of Honor, and Honorary Citizen and Friend of the Belgian Nation.)

After seeing Europe torn by hate, distrust, fear, and revenge, Hoover was relieved to return to the United States in 1919. In fact, Hoover was so glad to be home that he said he never wanted to see Europe again. More than before, he saw the United States as an island of moral leadership in a bloodstained world.

Wilson (seated, center) and his War Council; Hoover is standing, left.

Many people across the country also expressed their reaction against the war by saying the U.S. should reduce its involvement in international affairs and attend to domestic issues. Such an attitude became known as "isolationism." President Wilson campaigned across the country for acceptance of the Versailles Treaty with its provision for a League of Nations, an international organization designed to stop aggressors and head off future wars. Isolationists in the U.S. Senate, however, were afraid of too much involvement in foreign matters. They refused to vote the U.S. into the League, and Wilson refused to make

Wilson in Saint Louis in September 1919, speaking on behalf of the League of Nations

any compromises regarding the treaty. In the end, Wilson suffered a stroke in the middle of his cross-country tour, and the Senate rejected his Versailles Treaty altogether.

One commentator writing about the Versailles negotiations stated that Herbert Hoover was "the only man who emerged from the ordeal of Paris with an enhanced reputation. . . . This complex personality . . . [imparted to] the Councils of Paris . . . precisely that atmosphere of reality, knowledge, magnanimity and disinterestedness which, if they had been found in other quarters also, would have given us the Good Peace."

Chapter 5

Secretary of Commerce

When Hoover returned to the United States in 1919, he was so widely admired that both the Democrats and the Republicans were eyeing him as a presidential candidate. Franklin D. Roosevelt, who would end up being the Democratic candidate for vice-president in 1920, wrote about Hoover, "He is certainly a wonder and I wish we could make him President. There couldn't be a better one." Because of his role in postwar relief, Hoover could represent Wilson's idealism without sharing too much in his defeat. Hoover cut the Democrats short, however, by announcing his loyalty to the Republican party.

Progressive Republicans were all for Hoover, but the conservative Republican party bosses weren't interested in a candidate who was not a strong party man. For most of his career, Hoover had not even been in the country; moreover, he had worked closely with Democratic President Wilson and openly supported Wilson's plan for a League of Nations.

The Republicans chose mediocre, easygoing Warren G. Harding as their candidate. Harding promised a "return to normalcy." After the sacrifices of the war, Americans were ready to concentrate on material prosperity for a while. In a last surge of idealism, Congress passed the Eighteenth Amendment in January 1919, prohibiting alcoholic beverages. Not long after, people began to resent Prohibition. Speakeasies—private clubs where one could buy illegal alcohol—sprang up in the cities. Throughout the Roaring Twenties, gangsters like Chicago's Al Capone thrived on making and selling illegal liquor. Americans in the 1920s were not in the mood to deny themselves anything.

When Harding was elected by a huge majority, he asked Hoover to join his cabinet as secretary of commerce. Again, Republican party bosses were against the choice of Hoover. After some debate, they agreed, reasoning that the Department of Commerce was a relatively powerless backwater of government. People joked that the commerce department was in charge of "turning out the lighthouses at night and putting the fish to bed."

Hoover moved in with his usual energy and determination. He served as secretary of commerce for over seven years, first under Harding and then, after Harding's death in August 1923, under President Calvin Coolidge. During this time, newspaper cartoons showed swarms of Hoovers running around Washington, D.C. He seemed to be everywhere at once. A Washington reporter named Theodore Joslin wrote that Hoover was "the best single news source any of us had. . . . We found that an hour spent with him

Hoover's favorite cartoon, 1932

yielded enough news to give up a despatch a day for a week, with almost every one of them sure to make page one." Hoover constantly expanded his department's duties, increased its staff by three thousand employees, added over $13 million to its budget, and raised its prestige significantly.

Hoover, in Washington, D.C., being televised to New York viewers

Under Hoover, the Department of Commerce set policies that helped new technology become part of American life. Lighthouses started signaling ships with radio beacons. As more and more Americans bought their own radios, Hoover started holding annual radio industry conferences and made sure stations didn't overlap. To support the relatively new airline companies, Hoover urged the Post Office to send mail across the country in airplanes. At the same time, his department made flying safer by requiring all runways to have landing lights. In 1927, New Yorkers watched the first public demonstration of another new invention, television; the man on the screen was none other than Herbert Hoover.

The Commerce Department gave Hoover the perfect opportunity to put his ideas into practice. He was confident that American business could make a profit *and* be responsible to the workers. He saw himself leading the way to that middle ground between the extremes of cutthroat competition and socialist regulation. Most important of all, he was determined that business and industry would follow his lead voluntarily, without government interference and regulation. During the business boom of the Roaring Twenties, Hoover's ideals seemed within reach.

Under Hoover, the Commerce Department made it much easier for manufacturers to find new buyers for their goods. The Commerce Department began to publish lists of what manufacturers made and how much they had on hand. It published information on the population and buying power of every part of the U.S. Every month it published "What the World Wants," with information on what products foreign countries were buying.

The widespread use of this information encouraged manufacturers to standardize their products—that is, to make the same items, such as light bulbs or drainpipes or automobile tires, the same sizes. Customers could then fit a drainpipe made by one company into a section of pipe made by another firm. Standardizing products saved money for businesses and made life easier for consumers. Hoover said that a "man who has a standard automobile, a standard telephone, a standard bathtub, a standard electric light, a standard radio, and one and one-half hours less average daily labor is more of a man and has a fuller life and more individuality than he has without them."

Hoover Dam in 1936, in a spectacular night display

Hoover usually began his attack on a problem by calling a conference. He summoned experts and leaders to Washington to talk over problems such as unemployment, farm surpluses, child health, aviation, or water pollution. The next step was to get as much publicity as possible for the conference results. This would educate the public and put pressure on business, industry, and local government to take action. Sometimes Hoover's program worked spectacularly. He convinced seven western states to work together on building a huge dam, now called Hoover Dam, on the Colorado River.

He also persuaded the steel industry to go from a twelve- to an eight-hour workday. He enlisted the Federal Council of Churches and the press to help him promote the eight-hour day. Meanwhile, he worked behind the scenes, talking with industry leaders, getting President Harding to pressure them over dinner at the White House, and finally, publicly hailing their grudging promise to cut to eight-hour days. The industrialists' sense of decency had much less to do with the change than did their fear of bad publicity. However, they had cut the workday without being forced to do so by any law.

Hoover could also urge others into action on short notice. When a one-thousand-mile stretch of the Mississippi River flooded in 1927, Hoover organized a rescue effort involving 600 boats and 60 airplanes. He traveled to 91 towns getting them to set up camps for some of the 325,000 people flooded out of their homes. At each stop he made a brief speech: "A couple of thousand refugees are coming. They've got to have accommodations. Huts. Water-mains. Sewers. Streets. Dining-halls. Meals. Doctors. Everything. And you haven't got months to do it in. You haven't got weeks. You've got hours."

His programs didn't always work. Farm surpluses continued to drive prices down and hurt farmers; labor problems continued in the coal mining industry. A wave of unemployment hit the country from 1920 until 1922, but most congressmen were against trying to prevent future unemployment. Senator George Norris said, "We had better let God run [the economy] as in the past, and not take the power away from Him and give it to Hoover."

In 1928, whoever was running the economy seemed to be doing a good job. Business was riding a crest of unequaled prosperity. An ever-increasing number of Americans owned such consumer items as radios and cars. The Republican government could claim it had brought good times to the country.

When Republican president Calvin Coolidge decided not to run for a second term, Hoover was the natural candidate. After seven well-publicized years in the Commerce Department, Hoover was known all over the country as a dynamic and forward-looking leader, an ethical engineer who stood above political squabbling.

No one doubted that Hoover would win votes, but some Republicans were still wary of a man who never really had much to do with politics. Nevertheless, there was no stopping Hoover at the Republican national convention. He won the Republican nomination on the first ballot. On election day, he swept by his Democratic opponent, New York governor Al Smith, by an unprecedented majority, capturing 21,392,000 votes to Smith's 15,016,000.

Between his election and his inauguration, Hoover remarked, "My friends have made the American people think me a sort of superman, able to cope successfully with the most difficult and complicated problems. . . . They expect the impossible of me and should there arise in the land conditions with which the political machinery is unable to cope, I will be the one to suffer."

Within a year, the Great Depression would make Hoover's prediction come true; however, there was no hint of concern in his inaugural address. Amplifiers carried

Hoover with outgoing president Coolidge, going to Hoover's inauguration

Hoover's speech to the Washington, D.C., crowd of fifty thousand, while radios broadcast the address to millions more. Hoover said: "We want to see a nation built of homeowners and farmowners. We want to see their savings protected. We want to see them in steady jobs. . . . We want them all secure. . . . I have no fears for the future of our country. It is bright with hope."

Chapter 6

The Great Depression

Hoover launched into the presidency brimming with ideas. In contrast to Calvin Coolidge, "the least President America has ever had," Hoover began calling conferences on housing and child health and announcing commissions to study education and law enforcement. He pushed Congress to set aside money for buying up national park land, improving water transportation, reforming prisons, and providing better health care and education on American Indian reservations.

Early in his presidency, Hoover called a special session of Congress to help the country's farmers. Farmers had not shared in the overall prosperity of the 1920s. In fact, they were steadily losing ground as farm surpluses pushed prices lower and lower. During World War I, Hoover had urged farmers to produce more. Unfortunately, when demand dropped off after the war, farmers kept producing the extra food even though there were no buyers.

Individual farmers were afraid to grow less for fear they would lose money. Hoover reasoned that prices would go up only if farmers agreed to cut back their crops together.

In response to the farm crisis, Congress passed Hoover's Agricultural Marketing Act. The act did two things. First, it helped farmers set up cooperatives so that instead of competing with each other to sell their crops and paying middlemen to store and ship them, the farmers could band together to sell, store, and ship the food themselves. Second, the bill set up the Federal Farm Board to control surpluses and keep the food supply steady. This way, farmers could expect an even price for their goods. Hoover hoped that this new law would help the farmers join in the rest of the country's prosperity.

President Hoover did have one persistent worry about the boom — he kept warning against wild spending on the stock market. Usually people buy stock, or shares in a business, because they expect that when the business does well, they will get a dividend, or a share of the profits. Over the years, as the business grows and expands, the value of the stock should increase as well. As a result, the dividends can more than repay buyers for the money used to purchase their original stock.

In 1929, people were eager to buy stock. The push to buy made stock prices rise higher and higher. As prices rose, people started buying not to share in the business or to wait for dividends, but to sell for a quick profit as soon as the price of the stock went up.

In 1929, people bought and sold stocks over and over again, making a profit with every sale. This buying to make a quick sale is called speculation. Speculation is not based on the value of the stock but on the buyer's expectation of a quick profit.

New York traders relieved to find stocks rising the day after Black Tuesday

Worse yet, in the summer of 1929, many people were borrowing money to speculate in stock. The biggest investors weren't individuals speculating with their own savings; they were banks and trusts, speculating with the savings of thousands of people. The only problem with wild speculation is that as the prices get higher, the risk is greater. Stock market prices inflate like a bubble that threatens to burst at any time.

President Hoover tried to discourage speculation, but many of the New York bankers and stockbrokers were not willing to listen to him. When speculation becomes as heavy as it was in 1929, the prosperity cannot last. There has to come a day when investors get nervous and suddenly decide to sell their stocks. On October 29, 1929, the bubble finally burst, and the stock market crashed.

Prices had been sliding up and down for several weeks—enough to convince many investors that it was time to get their money out.

On October 29, called Black Tuesday, everyone who had been frantically buying wanted even more desperately to sell. Prices dropped sharply as over sixteen million shares were sold in a single day. People who bought stocks at high prices had to sell them for much less; many people who had borrowed money to buy stocks were financially ruined. Instead of tremendous profits, many faced overwhelming debts.

The crash ruined more than the investors. It destroyed the atmosphere of confidence and progress that had fueled the country's boom throughout the Roaring Twenties. Month by month, worried people started saving their money instead of spending it on new cars, clothes, or homes.

As spending dropped and products piled up unsold, businesses cut back on production. This meant that they needed fewer people, so thousands of factories, stores, and offices began laying off employees. Soon no one was hiring and no one was buying. The economy of the country ground slowly to a standstill, and the nation slid from

Anxious people across the street from the New York Stock Exchange in October 1929

prosperity into the start of the Great Depression. The same cycle of boom and bust had happened before in the country's history, but never on so large a scale and never for so long a time.

To get the economy moving again, someone was going to have to spend money. Farmers couldn't do it; they had been losing ground for years now, getting less and less return on their crops. Many of them were barely holding on to their farms. Many others had lost their farms and everything they owned.

Depression scene, Eastport, Maine, in August 1936

The industrial workers couldn't do it. All through the 1920s, wages had been rising but not nearly as fast as prices. The only way most workers could afford to buy new products such as washing machines or cars was on the installment plan. They paid only part of the cost at first and agreed to pay off the rest in installments, a little every month. Workers faced the beginning of the Great Depression loaded with debt. As wages spiraled down and unemployment rose, many workers sank into poverty.

The rich couldn't spend money. The tremendous business profits of the 1920s had flowed into the hands of a few wealthy owners. Instead of distributing the profits by increasing wages, many of these people had spent the money on stock speculation. Those who were not ruined by the crash were unwilling to put money into wages and production when there was no one to buy their products.

The Bank of the United States in New York City closes its doors.

Bankers had no money to spend. Many of the largest New York banks had invested heavily in the stock market. In the crash, they lost the savings of thousands and thousands of people. Before the banks could earn the money back again, people panicked and began to withdraw their savings from the banks. Some banks simply didn't have enough cash to give everyone; the money was tied up in loans to businesses, to home owners, and to foreign countries. When a bank ran out of money, it closed for good, leaving people no hope of getting back their savings.

Across the country, millions of helpless, angry, and debt-ridden people turned to Hoover for help. Maybe the government could put enough money into the economy to start things up again. Hoover had saved Belgium and practically all of Europe from chaos and starvation. Surely now he could stop a depression in his own country.

Chapter 7

President Reject

No president before Hoover had felt that government needed to do much about a depression. It was simply a natural part of economic life, something like the weather. Hoover's secretary of the treasury, millionaire Andrew Mellon, was a *laissez-faire* conservative who believed that a depression wasn't all bad. "People will work harder, live a more moral life. Values will be adjusted, and enterprising people will pick up the wrecks from less competent people." A surprising number of congressmen, bankers, and industrialists shared Mellon's opinion.

Hoover did not. He would not stand by and watch the economy sink. His ideas about voluntary cooperation and scientific management had worked in crises before; he was confident that they would work this time.

Always before—in the CRB, in the Food Administration, even in the Department of Commerce—Hoover had insisted on having a free hand. Now he had to argue every measure through an uncooperative Congress. When Hoover asked for a mild tariff reform chiefly to protect American farmers from lower-priced foreign products, Congress debated for months before coming up with the Smoot-Hawley Bill, which instituted whopping tariff increases across the board.

Andrew Mellon, secretary of the treasury for both Coolidge and Hoover

Hoover expected Congress to put politics aside to deal with the Depression. Instead, congressional Democrats saw that they had a chance to oust the Republicans from power. Meanwhile Hoover's own party was so divided that a prominent group of progressive Republican congressmen were as likely to vote *against* Hoover as with him.

Acting on his own, Hoover got a group of prominent industrialists to agree that they would not cut wages. If business was ever to get back on its feet, consumers would have to have enough money to buy products. The businessmen agreed, and they mostly kept their word for the next two years. This was a bold step, but it didn't work for long.

At first, instead of cutting everyone's pay, companies kept some people at their usual pay and laid off others. Those who still had jobs saved as much of their pay as they could, because they feared the day when they too would be without work.

By the fall of 1931, two years after the crash, the Depression was worse than ever. Big employers—such as U.S. Steel and Ford—began to feel that they could no longer hold the line. They began to cut wages. Small companies quickly followed suit.

Hoover's Federal Farm Board set out to protect farmers from the worst of the crash by buying up farm products. By 1931, the Farm Board had bought up 257 million bushels of wheat with no buyers in sight. Hoover had no choice but to give away this huge surplus to the mass of poor and unemployed. After losing $345 million, the Farm Board had to stop. Its actions were driving farm prices even lower. A bushel of wheat, which had cost $1.02 in 1929, cost 37 cents in 1932; a bushel of corn dropped from 91 cents to 31 cents.

As secretary of commerce, Hoover had worked to build foreign markets for American crops, but in 1931, Europe couldn't afford to buy. Germany and Austria were paying off huge war reparations, while France, Britain, and others owed tremendous war debts.

Just as it seemed that things were improving in the United States, the Austrian and German banking system collapsed under its debts. This European crash threatened lenders and investors all over the world, including many American banks.

Hoover and his wife, Lou, in Cleveland in 1930

Hoover had an idea that prevented a world financial disaster. He suggested a year's moratorium on international war debts and reparations. Moreover, he successfully convinced world leaders and the U.S. Congress to back up his ideas. His bold action bought time for the U.S. and Europe to hold off total ruin, but Europe was still not strong enough to help the U.S. out of its depression.

Hoover persuaded Congress to vote for his Reconstruction Finance Corporation (RFC), an organization designed to bail out small banks that were in trouble. The RFC did slow down the rate of bank failures. Within six months, the RFC had lent over $1 billion. Hoover firmly believed that money given to institutions such as banks would filter down through the economy, creating confidence and, eventually, jobs. On the other hand, he feared that giving money directly to the needy would create a whole class of people who depended on the government for survival.

Three of the fifteen men who lived in a shack in this New York City junk yard, 1932

Hoover still clung to his idea that government should help people to help themselves. But as the Depression dragged on, Hoover's ideals of self-help and voluntary cooperation lost their appeal for jobless, homeless, and hungry Americans. By 1933, one-fourth of the country's workers were unemployed. Near every big city, homeless people were building shanty towns, rows of haphazard shacks built out of scraps of lumber, tin, cardboard, and any other materials the builders could find. People called these ramshackle settlements "Hoovervilles." Likewise, turning empty pockets inside out to show that you had no money was called "waving Hooverflags." Herbert Hoover — one of the most popular presidents ever elected — was rapidly becoming one of the most hated men in the country.

Federal American National Bank president John Poole tells panic-stricken depositors that all is well (Washington, D.C., 1931).

To help build national confidence, Hoover kept issuing hopeful statements from the White House. For example, right after the crash, he said, "The fundamental business of the country . . . is on a sound and prosperous basis." But his statements failed to cheer anyone up. Instead they backfired and made people believe that Hoover had no idea how much they were suffering. Hoover also felt he had to conceal much of the information that came to him, such as which banks were in trouble or how much gold was leaving the country, to avoid further panic. Unfortunately, this led people to think of him as a do-nothing.

On the contrary, Hoover and his staff were working long, grueling hours. Hoover's days were filled with meetings and conferences, and he often managed on only a few hours of sleep a night. He refused to take vacations and cut down his public appearances. Instead of chatting with White House visitors, Hoover would stroll out to the grounds at an appointed time to take his place among groups that were already posed for a picture.

He refused to let newspapers write about his human side. When Hoover learned that three Detroit children had hitchhiked to Washington to ask him to get their father out of jail, he told his secretary, "Three children resourceful enough to manage to get to Washington to see me are going to see me." After a private interview with the children, Hoover, near tears, ordered their father to be released. He also made sure this story never appeared in print.

What people did see was the formal-dress dinner parties that he and Lou hosted night after night. Although he was often reserved and silent during these dinners, Hoover loved dinner company. The Hoovers' formality allowed him to enjoy people without having to make much small talk. The image of Hoover in a tuxedo and smoking a cigar over an elegant table made him look remote from the people's sufferings. They forgot about the Great Humanitarian and instead remembered that Hoover was himself a wealthy man. Even his most creative responses to the Depression—the moratorium on European debt and the Reconstruction Finance Corporation—had people saying that Hoover was willing to help banks and foreigners but he wouldn't lift a finger for ordinary people.

In spite of his engineer's detachment and scientific outlook, Hoover's feelings were easily hurt by all the bad publicity. He withdrew even further from the public and worked harder. When he was nominated for a second term by an unenthusiastic Republican party, he announced that he would be too busy running the country to campaign much. In the past, Herbert Hoover had never been one to give in when he believed he was right. Now when the country turned against him, he dug in harder.

By 1932, when Americans were calling for help from Washington, Hoover was asking Congress to raise taxes to keep the federal government from going deeply into debt. "We cannot thus squander ourselves into prosperity," he said. Meanwhile, members of Congress were trying to win votes at home by putting forward various relief bills. Hoover calculated that all together these bills would cost the federal government $40 billion.

One bill before Congress in summer 1932 was called the Bonus Bill. World War I veterans were scheduled to receive a bonus payment in 1945. The Bonus Bill demanded early payment of this money. Hoover had made generous provisions for veterans, but he felt this bill was a huge expense that wouldn't help the country's neediest people. As the Bonus Bill came up for a vote, destitute veterans swarmed into Washington with their wives and children to demonstrate for the bill. The Bonus Army, as this collection of about twenty thousand people was called, moved into abandoned buildings in downtown Washington and built camps of makeshift shacks across a bridge from downtown in an area called the Anacostia Flats.

The Bonus Army marches on the Capitol

On July 15, the Bonus Bill was defeated in the Senate. Hoover approved a bill giving the disappointed Bonus Army veterans enough money to go home. Several thousand of them stayed, however, living in cluttered, unsanitary camps, cooking cans of beans on the city sidewalks, and demonstrating for additional relief money.

When Washington police tried to clear the veterans from a building that was supposed to be destroyed, a riot broke out. The police could not contain thousands of angry protesters, and city authorities asked Hoover for help from the U.S. Army. Hoover sent in General Douglas MacArthur with orders to guide the veterans out of the city, back across the river to their camp. Women and children were to be treated kindly.

Bonus marchers parading from the Washington Monument to the Capitol

MacArthur charged in with tear gas bombs and tanks. Troopers with bayonets drove the crowd out of the city and, against Hoover's direct orders, followed them across the bridge, burning the Anacostia camp to ashes. A seven-year-old boy who tried to go back to his hut for his pet rabbit was stabbed in the leg; an injured infant had to be rushed to a hospital and later died. Newspapers carried the story everywhere, and readers were shocked to see how heartlessly the ex-soldiers were being treated.

Soldiers with gas masks and fixed bayonets battle the bonus-seekers.

Hoover never publicly criticized MacArthur for his outright disobedience. As a result, the president took the blame. One magazine wrote, "Hoover's campaign for reelection was launched Thursday, July 28, . . . with 4 troops of cavalry, 4 companies of infantry, a mounted machine-gun squadron, six whippet tanks, 300 city policemen and a squad of Secret Service men and Treasury Agents." The Democratic presidential candidate, Franklin D. Roosevelt, commented to a friend, "Well, Felix, this elects me."

77

Chapter 8

Innocent Bystander

In the 1928 campaign, a Republican slogan promised "A Chicken in Every Pot, Two Cars in Every Garage." In 1932, Hoover's campaign for reelection hinged on defending actions that most people didn't know about and didn't understand. "Let no man tell you it could not be worse. It could be so much worse that these days now, distressing as they are, would look like veritable prosperity," he said.

His flat, monotonous speaking voice; his ponderous, fact-crammed speeches; and his grim, lined face compared unfavorably with the fluid voice, resounding speeches, and light-hearted manner of Franklin D. Roosevelt. The two didn't differ much on basic issues — Roosevelt had no firm program in mind to deal with the Depression. However, Hoover seemed to represent the failure of the past and Roosevelt the hope of the future.

On election day, only six of the forty-eight states went for Hoover. The *New York Times* called him a "President Reject." One commentator wrote, "Only when a decade or more had passed, would Americans be able to divine for themselves whether Hoover was 'the last routed defender of the old order or a leader born before his time.' "

Opposite page: Herbert and Lou
at the White House in 1932

Hoover and President-Elect Roosevelt on the way to FDR's inauguration

Herbert Hoover and Franklin D. Roosevelt rode together to Roosevelt's inauguration on March 4, 1933. The two men did not get along. Roosevelt's refusal to work with Hoover between the election and the inauguration allowed the country to slide into a dangerous banking crisis. Roosevelt would later address this crisis by declaring a nationwide bank holiday, closing all banks for a few days. On this gray and gusty day, the two men had little to say to one another.

The Hoovers' home on the Stanford University campus in Palo Alto, California

After the ceremonies, Hoover and Lou went by train to the Waldorf-Astoria Hotel in New York. Hoover wanted to be close by to receive any calls from Washington, but none came. Roosevelt never consulted Hoover nor tried to involve him in government in any way. After a few weeks, the Hoovers traveled crosscountry to their home in Palo Alto, California, where Hoover kept up with events by reading thirty newspapers a day. Hoover didn't like what he read. In 1934, he published his second book, *The Challenge to Liberty*, an attack on Roosevelt's "New Deal" economic policies.

First Lady Lou Henry Hoover

In spring 1933, Roosevelt's secretary of the interior, Harold Ickes, changed the name on the huge dam being built on the Colorado River from Hoover Dam to Boulder Dam, despite the fact that Hoover had spent years as secretary of commerce to get the project started. Roosevelt didn't reverse his secretary's petty decision; Hoover was not even invited to the opening ceremonies in 1935. Roosevelt did break the silence between them to send a telegram of condolence when Lou Henry Hoover died of a heart attack in 1944. After her death, Hoover made his permanent home in Suite 31-A in the Waldorf-Astoria.

Though he had never had close ties to his political party while in office, Hoover became a staunch Republican in the long thirty-one years of his retirement. The Republican party offered a means for Hoover to voice his opposition to Roosevelt's New Deal. Hoover warned that Roosevelt was replacing voluntary community action with a vast federal bureaucracy, and that instead of working with their neighbors, people were learning to depend on the national government to solve problems. Ironically, many of Roosevelt's New Deal ideas originated in the Hoover presidency. When a friend once said to Hoover, "I have a suspicion that you would have signed practically all the legislation that F.D.R. signed," Hoover answered, "I think I would have."

Every four years, he addressed the Republican convention, receiving long ovations. But every year he was disappointed to find that even his own party did not accept his ideas. In 1936, Hoover was plainly available for the presidential nomination, but the convention instead chose Alfred Landon. Landon did not even want Hoover to make speeches in his behalf. For years Hoover spoke and wrote in political isolation. For years, every Democratic politician talked as if he were running against Hoover.

After Roosevelt's death, President Harry Truman invited Hoover to the White House on May 28, 1945. Truman remembered that Hoover had tears in his eyes. It was the first time he had been in the White House since Roosevelt's inauguration, twelve years earlier. Hoover and Truman liked one another and maintained their friendship for many years.

Former President Hoover addressing the 1936 Republican national convention

When Truman was searching for someone to organize European war relief after World War II, the most experienced man in the country was the seventy-three-year-old Hoover. "I have a job for you that nobody else in the country can do," Truman told Hoover. In 1946, Hoover traveled to thirty-eight countries in an unpressurized plane that he nicknamed *The Flying Cow*, doing a familiar job—documenting food needs, finding surpluses, and arranging to ship food to needy countries.

President Truman conferring with Hoover about feeding the overseas needy

In 1947, Truman appointed Hoover the chairman of the Commission on Organization of the Executive Branch of the Government. Since 1921, Hoover had been trying to streamline the apparatus of the federal government. Congress refused to go along with his suggestions during the Depression; but after government jobs and expenses grew under Roosevelt, everyone could see that it was time to cut out waste and improve efficiency. With a staff of 300 experts, Hoover set to work and came up with 273 recommendations. The time was right. Truman put three-fourths of them into effect, and the government saved billions of dollars. Also during Truman's administration, in 1947, Congress passed a bill renaming the Colorado River dam "Hoover Dam."

Hoover (front, left) applauds at Dwight D. Eisenhower's inauguration in 1953. Eisenhower shakes hands with outgoing president Truman, as Eisenhower's vice-president, Richard Nixon (right), looks on.

In 1952, Dwight D. Eisenhower became the first Republican since Hoover to win the presidency. Hoover attended the inauguration, his first since 1933. Now in his eighties, Hoover had outlived the people's undeserved bitterness toward him. Although presidents Eisenhower, Kennedy, and Johnson weren't always willing to follow Hoover's advice, they were eager to hear what he had to say. Eisenhower made Hoover chairman of a second commission on government reform but only put into effect a third of the commission's recommendations. This position was Hoover's last public office.

His remaining years he spent writing several books. They included *American Epic*, about relief movements in Europe; *The Ordeal of Woodrow Wilson*, about Wilson's experience in working on the Versailles Treaty; and the unpublished manuscript *Freedom Betrayed*, about failures in American foreign policy.

He continued to raise funds and to keep an eye on Stanford University's Hoover Institution on War, Revolution, and Peace. Hoover had founded this research library back in his Belgian relief days. He had given Stanford his tremendous collection of documents that he had gathered in Europe during World War I.

In 1958, at Eisenhower's request, Hoover represented the U.S. on the July 4 celebration at the Brussels World's Fair. Hoover and one widow were the only CRB members left alive. In 1960, he addressed his eighth and last Republican nominating convention. This time the Republicans nominated Richard M. Nixon to oppose John F. Kennedy. In his farewell speech to the delegates, he said, "Unless some miracle comes to me from the Good Lord, this is finally it."

In 1962 Hoover made his last fishing trip to Key Largo, Florida. Fishing had been a favorite sport ever since his Iowa boyhood. During his hardworking presidency, fishing at his camp on Virginia's Rapidan River had been the only relaxation Hoover allowed himself. On this 1962 trip, he gave away his rod and reel, feeling that he would not have the strength to return. That August, he was too ill to last through the dedication ceremonies of the new Hoover Library in West Branch, Iowa.

In October 1964, an ulcer just above Hoover's stomach began bleeding and couldn't be stopped. At ninety, Hoover was too old for surgery. His sons Allan and Herbert, Jr., stayed with him in Suite 31-A to follow his "rugged fight." Herbert Hoover died midday on October 20, 1964.

A blacksmith's son in the age of horses and buggies, Hoover had lived to see an astronaut orbit the earth. Perhaps the greatest change Hoover lived through was his own country's attitude toward himself and his ideals. The same ideas—scientific efficiency in government, voluntary cooperation to solve problems—were hailed as marks of progressive and modern leadership when he was swept into the presidency in 1928. Four years later, in the depths of the Great Depression, Americans angrily rejected Hoover and his ideas as heartlessly inadequate.

The voters' rejection of Hoover might not have been so strong if they hadn't expected so much of him in the first place. Back in 1932, one commentator said, "Hoover will be known as the greatest innocent bystander in history . . . full of courage and patriotism, undaunted to the last . . . a brave man fighting valiantly, futilely to the end."

By 1964, the country and its government had changed so much that there was no going back to the ideals Hoover still valued. People did begin to see, however, that Hoover had correctly predicted the dangers that would follow the expanded government powers of Roosevelt's New Deal and the problems in foreign relations brought on by World War II. Most people still see Hoover's presidency as a failure, although they don't blame its failure on the president

Herbert Hoover in 1962 at the age of eighty-eight

alone. By the time of his death, people no longer doubted that Hoover had loved his country deeply and labored to his utmost for the people's welfare.

After his death thousands of mourners filed by his casket, on view first in New York City, then in the Capitol in Washington, D.C., and finally in West Branch, Iowa, where Hoover lies buried. A Quaker friend said of him in a simple eulogy, "He has worked hard; he has been very brave; he has endured."

Chronology of American History

(Shaded area covers events in Herbert Hoover's lifetime.)

About A.D. 982—Eric the Red, born in Norway, reaches Greenland in one of the first European voyages to North America.

About 985—Eric the Red brings settlers from Iceland to Greenland.

About 1000—Leif Ericson (Eric the Red's son) leads what is thought to be the first European expedition to mainland North America; Leif probably lands in Canada.

1492—Christopher Columbus, seeking a sea route from Spain to the Far East, discovers the New World.

1497—John Cabot reaches Canada in the first English voyage to North America.

1513—Ponce de Léon explores Florida in search of the fabled Fountain of Youth.

1519-1521—Hernando Cortés of Spain conquers Mexico.

1534—French explorers led by Jacques Cartier enter the Gulf of St. Lawrence in Canada.

1540—Spanish explorer Francisco Coronado begins exploring the American Southwest, seeking the riches of the mythical Seven Cities of Cibola.

1565—St. Augustine, Florida, the first permanent European town in what is now the United States, is founded by the Spanish.

1607—Jamestown, Virginia, is founded, the first permanent English town in the present-day U.S.

1608—Frenchman Samuel de Champlain founds the village of Quebec, Canada.

1609—Henry Hudson explores the eastern coast of present-day U.S. for the Netherlands; the Dutch then claim parts of New York, New Jersey, Delaware, and Connecticut and name the area New Netherland.

1619—The English colonies' first shipment of black slaves arrives in Jamestown.

1620—English Pilgrims found Massachusetts' first permanent town at Plymouth.

1621—Massachusetts Pilgrims and Indians hold the famous first Thanksgiving feast in colonial America.

1623—Colonization of New Hampshire is begun by the English.

1624—Colonization of present-day New York State is begun by the Dutch at Fort Orange (Albany).

1625—The Dutch start building New Amsterdam (now New York City).

1630—The town of Boston, Massachusetts, is founded by the English Puritans.

1633—Colonization of Connecticut is begun by the English.

1634—Colonization of Maryland is begun by the English.

1636—Harvard, the colonies' first college, is founded in Massachusetts. Rhode Island colonization begins when Englishman Roger Williams founds Providence.

1638—Delaware colonization begins when Swedish people build Fort Christina at present-day Wilmington.

1640—Stephen Daye of Cambridge, Massachusetts prints *The Bay Psalm Book*, the first English-language book published in what is now the U.S.

1643—Swedish settlers begin colonizing Pennsylvania.

About 1650—North Carolina is colonized by Virginia settlers.

1660—New Jersey colonization is begun by the Dutch at present-day Jersey City.

1670—South Carolina colonization is begun by the English near Charleston.

1673—Jacques Marquette and Louis Jolliet explore the upper Mississippi River for France.

1682—Philadelphia, Pennsylvania, is settled. La Salle explores Mississippi River all the way to its mouth in Louisiana and claims the whole Mississippi Valley for France.

1693—College of William and Mary is founded in Williamsburg, Virginia.

1700—Colonial population is about 250,000.

1703—Benjamin Franklin is born in Boston.

1732—George Washington, first president of the U.S., is born in Westmoreland County, Virginia.

1733—James Oglethorpe founds Savannah, Georgia; Georgia is established as the thirteenth colony.

1735—John Adams, second president of the U.S., is born in Braintree, Massachusetts.

1737—William Byrd founds Richmond, Virginia.

1738—British troops are sent to Georgia over border dispute with Spain.

1739—Black insurrection takes place in South Carolina.

1740—English Parliament passes act allowing naturalization of immigrants to American colonies after seven-year residence.

1743—Thomas Jefferson, third president of the U.S., is born in Albemarle County, Virginia. Benjamin Franklin retires at age thirty-seven to devote himself to scientific inquiries and public service.

1744—King George's War begins; France joins war effort against England.

1745—During King George's War, France raids settlements in Maine and New York.

1747—Classes begin at Princeton College in New Jersey.

1748—The Treaty of Aix-la-Chapelle concludes King George's War.

1749—Parliament legally recognizes slavery in colonies and the inauguration of the plantation system in the South. George Washington becomes the surveyor for Culpepper County in Virginia.

1750—Thomas Walker passes through and names Cumberland Gap on his way toward Kentucky region. Colonial population is about 1,200,000.

1751—James Madison, fourth president of the U.S., is born in Port Conway, Virginia. English Parliament passes Currency Act, banning New England colonies from issuing paper money. George Washington travels to Barbados.

1752—Pennsylvania Hospital, the first general hospital in the colonies, is founded in Philadelphia. Benjamin Franklin uses a kite in a thunderstorm to demonstrate that lightning is a form of electricity.

1753—George Washington delivers command from Virginia Lieutenant Governor Dinwiddie that the French withdraw from the Ohio River Valley; French disregard the demand. Colonial population is about 1,328,000.

1754—French and Indian War begins (extends to Europe as the Seven Years' War). Washington surrenders at Fort Necessity.

1755—French and Indians ambush General Braddock. Washington becomes commander of Virginia troops.

1756—England declares war on France.

1758—James Monroe, fifth president of the U.S., is born in Westmoreland County, Virginia.

1759—Cherokee Indian war begins in southern colonies; hostilities extend to 1761. George Washington marries Martha Dandridge Custis.

1760—George III becomes king of England. Colonial population is about 1,600,000.

1762—England declares war on Spain.

1763—Treaty of Paris concludes the French and Indian War and the Seven Years' War. England gains Canada and most other French lands east of the Mississippi River.

1764—British pass the Sugar Act to gain tax money from the colonists. The issue of taxation without representation is first introduced in Boston. John Adams marries Abigail Smith.

1765—Stamp Act goes into effect in the colonies. Business virtually stops as almost all colonists refuse to use the stamps.

1766—British repeal the Stamp Act.

1767—John Quincy Adams, sixth president of the U.S. and son of second president John Adams, is born in Braintree, Massachusetts. Andrew Jackson, seventh president of the U.S., is born in Waxhaw settlement, South Carolina.

1769—Daniel Boone sights the Kentucky Territory.

1770—In the Boston Massacre, British soldiers kill five colonists and injure six. Townshend Acts are repealed, thus eliminating all duties on imports to the colonies except tea.

1771—Benjamin Franklin begins his autobiography, a work that he will never complete. The North Carolina assembly passes the "Bloody Act," which makes rioters guilty of treason.

1772—Samuel Adams rouses colonists to consider British threats to self-government. Thomas Jefferson marries Martha Wayles Skelton.

1773—English Parliament passes the Tea Act. Colonists dressed as Mohawk Indians board British tea ships and toss 342 casks of tea into the water in what becomes known as the Boston Tea Party. William Henry Harrison is born in Charles City County, Virginia.

1774—British close the port of Boston to punish the city for the Boston Tea Party. First Continental Congress convenes in Philadelphia.

1775—American Revolution begins with battles of Lexington and Concord, Massachusetts. Second Continental Congress opens in Philadelphia. George Washington becomes commander-in-chief of the Continental army.

1776—Declaration of Independence is adopted on July 4.

1777—Congress adopts the American flag with thirteen stars and thirteen stripes. John Adams is sent to France to negotiate peace treaty.

1778—France declares war against Great Britain and becomes U.S. ally.

1779—British surrender to Americans at Vincennes. Thomas Jefferson is elected governor of Virginia. James Madison is elected to the Continental Congress.

1780—Benedict Arnold, first American traitor, defects to the British.

1781—Articles of Confederation go into effect. Cornwallis surrenders to George Washington at Yorktown, ending the American Revolution.

1782—American commissioners, including John Adams, sign peace treaty with British in Paris. Thomas Jefferson's wife, Martha, dies. Martin Van Buren is born in Kinderhook, New York.

1784—Zachary Taylor is born near Barboursville, Virginia.

1785—Congress adopts the dollar as the unit of currency. John Adams is made minister to Great Britain. Thomas Jefferson is appointed minister to France.

1786—Shays' Rebellion begins in Massachusetts.

1787—Constitutional Convention assembles in Philadelphia, with George Washington presiding; U.S. Constitution is adopted. Delaware, New Jersey, and Pennsylvania become states.

1788—Virginia, South Carolina, New York, Connecticut, New Hampshire, Maryland, and Massachusetts become states. U.S. Constitution is ratified. New York City is declared U.S. capital.

1789—Presidential electors elect George Washington and John Adams as first president and vice-president. Thomas Jefferson is appointed secretary of state. North Carolina becomes a state. French Revolution begins.

1790—Supreme Court meets for the first time. Rhode Island becomes a state. First national census in the U.S. counts 3,929,214 persons. John Tyler is born in Charles City County, Virginia.

1791—Vermont enters the Union. U.S. Bill of Rights, the first ten amendments to the Constitution, goes into effect. District of Columbia is established.

1792—Thomas Paine publishes *The Rights of Man*. Kentucky becomes a state. Two political parties are formed in the U.S., Federalist and Republican. Washington is elected to a second term, with Adams as vice-president.

1793—War between France and Britain begins; U.S. declares neutrality. Eli Whitney invents the cotton gin; cotton production and slave labor increase in the South.

1794—Eleventh Amendment to the Constitution is passed, limiting federal courts' power. "Whiskey Rebellion" in Pennsylvania protests federal whiskey tax. James Madison marries Dolley Payne Todd.

1795—George Washington signs the Jay Treaty with Great Britain. Treaty of San Lorenzo, between U.S. and Spain, settles Florida boundary and gives U.S. right to navigate the Mississippi. James Polk is born near Pineville, North Carolina.

1796—Tennessee enters the Union. Washington gives his Farewell Address, refusing a third presidential term. John Adams is elected president and Thomas Jefferson vice-president.

1797—Adams recommends defense measures against possible war with France. Napoleon Bonaparte and his army march against Austrians in Italy. U.S. population is about 4,900,000.

1798—Washington is named commander-in-chief of the U.S. army. Department of the Navy is created. Alien and Sedition Acts are passed. Napoleon's troops invade Egypt and Switzerland.

1799—George Washington dies at Mount Vernon. James Monroe is elected governor of Virginia. French Revolution ends. Napoleon becomes ruler of France.

1800—Thomas Jefferson and Aaron Burr tie for president. U.S. capital is moved from Philadelphia to Washington, D.C. The White House is built as presidents' home. Spain returns Louisiana to France. Millard Fillmore is born in Locke, New York.

1801—After thirty-six ballots, House of Representatives elects Thomas Jefferson president, making Burr vice-president. James Madison is named secretary of state.

1802—Congress abolishes excise taxes. U.S. Military Academy is founded at West Point, New York.

1803—Ohio enters the Union. Louisiana Purchase treaty is signed with France, greatly expanding U.S. territory.

1804—Twelfth Amendment to the Constitution rules that president and vice-president be elected separately. Alexander Hamilton is killed by Vice-President Aaron Burr in a duel. Orleans Territory is established. Napoleon crowns himself emperor of France.

1805—Thomas Jefferson begins his second term as president. Lewis and Clark expedition reaches the Pacific Ocean.

1806—Coinage of silver dollars is stopped; resumes in 1836.

1807—Aaron Burr is acquitted in treason trial. Embargo Act closes U.S. ports to trade.

1808—James Madison is elected president. Congress outlaws importing slaves from Africa.

1810—U.S. population is 7,240,000.

1811—William Henry Harrison defeats Indians at Tippecanoe. Monroe is named secretary of state.

1812—Louisiana becomes a state. U.S. declares war on Britain (War of 1812). James Madison is reelected president. Napoleon invades Russia.

1813—British forces take Fort Niagara and Buffalo, New York.

1814—Francis Scott Key writes "The Star-Spangled Banner." British troops burn much of Washington, D.C., including the White House. Treaty of Ghent ends War of 1812. James Monroe becomes secretary of war.

1815—Napoleon meets his final defeat at Battle of Waterloo.

1816—James Monroe is elected president. Indiana becomes a state.

1817—Mississippi becomes a state. Construction on Erie Canal begins.

1821—Missouri enters the Union as a slave state. Santa Fe Trail opens the American Southwest. Mexico declares independence from Spain. Napoleon Bonaparte dies.

1822—U.S. recognizes Mexico and Colombia. Liberia in Africa is founded as a home for freed slaves. Ulysses S. Grant is born in Point Pleasant, Ohio. Rutherford B. Hayes is born in Delaware, Ohio.

1823—Monroe Doctrine closes North and South America to European colonizing or invasion.

1824—House of Representatives elects John Quincy Adams president when none of the four candidates wins a majority in national election. Mexico becomes a republic.

1825—Erie Canal is opened. U.S. population is 11,300,000.

1826—Thomas Jefferson and John Adams both die on July 4, the fiftieth anniversary of the Declaration of Independence.

1828—Andrew Jackson is elected president. Tariff of Abominations is passed, cutting imports.

1829—James Madison attends Virginia's constitutional convention. Slavery is abolished in Mexico. Chester A. Arthur is born in Fairfield, Vermont.

1830—Indian Removal Act to resettle Indians west of the Mississippi is approved.

1831—James Monroe dies in New York City. James A. Garfield is born in Orange, Ohio. Cyrus McCormick develops his reaper.

1832—Andrew Jackson, nominated by the new Democratic Party, is reelected president.

1833—Britain abolishes slavery in its colonies. Benjamin Harrison is born in North Bend, Ohio.

1835—Federal government becomes debt-free for the first time.

1836—Martin Van Buren becomes president. Texas wins independence from Mexico. Arkansas joins the Union. James Madison dies at Montpelier, Virginia.

1837—Michigan enters the Union. U.S. population is 15,900,000. Grover Cleveland is born in Caldwell, New Jersey.

1840—William Henry Harrison is elected president.

1841—President Harrison dies in Washington, D.C., one month after inauguration. Vice-President John Tyler succeeds him.

1843—William McKinley is born in Niles, Ohio.

1844—James Knox Polk is elected president. Samuel Morse sends first telegraphic message.

1845—Texas and Florida become states. Potato famine in Ireland causes massive emigration from Ireland to U.S. Andrew Jackson dies near Nashville, Tennessee.

1846—Iowa enters the Union. War with Mexico begins.

1847—U.S. captures Mexico City.

1848—John Quincy Adams dies in Washington, D.C. Zachary Taylor becomes president. Treaty of Guadalupe Hidalgo ends Mexico-U.S. war. Wisconsin becomes a state.

1849—James Polk dies in Nashville, Tennessee.

1850—President Taylor dies in Washington, D.C.; Vice-President Millard Fillmore succeeds him. California enters the Union, breaking tie between slave and free states.

1852—Franklin Pierce is elected president.

1853—Gadsden Purchase transfers Mexican territory to U.S.

1854—"War for Bleeding Kansas" is fought between slave and free states.

1855—Czar Nicholas I of Russia dies, succeeded by Alexander II.

1856—James Buchanan is elected president. In Massacre of Potawatomi Creek, Kansas-slavers are murdered by free-staters. Woodrow Wilson is born in Staunton, Virginia.

1857—William Howard Taft is born in Cincinnati, Ohio.

1858—Minnesota enters the Union. Theodore Roosevelt is born in New York City.

1859—Oregon becomes a state.

1860—Abraham Lincoln is elected president; South Carolina secedes from the Union in protest.

1861—Arkansas, Tennessee, North Carolina, and Virginia secede. Kansas enters the Union as a free state. Civil War begins.

1862—Union forces capture Fort Henry, Roanoke Island, Fort Donelson, Jacksonville, and New Orleans; Union armies are defeated at the battles of Bull Run and Fredericksburg. Martin Van Buren dies in Kinderhook, New York. John Tyler dies near Charles City, Virginia.

1863—Lincoln issues Emancipation Proclamation: all slaves held in rebelling territories are declared free. West Virginia becomes a state.

1864—Abraham Lincoln is reelected. Nevada becomes a state.

1865—Lincoln is assassinated in Washington, D.C., and succeeded by Andrew Johnson. U.S. Civil War ends on May 26. Thirteenth Amendment abolishes slavery. Warren G. Harding is born in Blooming Grove, Ohio.

1867—Nebraska becomes a state. U.S. buys Alaska from Russia for $7,200,000. Reconstruction Acts are passed.

1868—President Johnson is impeached for violating Tenure of Office Act, but is acquitted by Senate. Ulysses S. Grant is elected president. Fourteenth Amendment prohibits voting discrimination. James Buchanan dies in Lancaster, Pennsylvania.

1869—Franklin Pierce dies in Concord, New Hampshire.

1870—Fifteenth Amendment gives blacks the right to vote.

1872—Grant is reelected over Horace Greeley. General Amnesty Act pardons ex-Confederates. Calvin Coolidge is born in Plymouth Notch, Vermont.

1874—Millard Fillmore dies in Buffalo, New York. Herbert Hoover is born in West Branch, Iowa.

1875—Andrew Johnson dies in Carter's Station, Tennessee.

1876—Colorado enters the Union. "Custer's last stand": he and his men are massacred by Sioux Indians at Little Big Horn, Montana.

1877—Rutherford B. Hayes is elected president as all disputed votes are awarded to him.

1880—James A. Garfield is elected president.

1881—President Garfield is assassinated and dies in Elberon, New Jersey. Vice-President Chester A. Arthur succeeds him.

1882—U.S. bans Chinese immigration. Franklin D. Roosevelt is born in Hyde Park, New York.

1884—Grover Cleveland is elected president. Harry S. Truman is born in Lamar, Missouri.

1885—Ulysses S. Grant dies in Mount McGregor, New York.

1886—Statue of Liberty is dedicated. Chester A. Arthur dies in New York City.

1888—Benjamin Harrison is elected president.

1889—North Dakota, South Dakota, Washington, and Montana become states.

1890—Dwight D. Eisenhower is born in Denison, Texas. Idaho and Wyoming become states.

1892—Grover Cleveland is elected president.

1893—Rutherford B. Hayes dies in Fremont, Ohio.

1896—William McKinley is elected president. Utah becomes a state.

1898—U.S. declares war on Spain over Cuba.

1900—McKinley is reelected. Boxer Rebellion against foreigners in China begins.

1901—McKinley is assassinated by anarchist Leon Czolgosz in Buffalo, New York; Theodore Roosevelt becomes president. Benjamin Harrison dies in Indianapolis, Indiana.

1902—U.S. acquires perpetual control over Panama Canal.

1903—Alaskan frontier is settled.

1904—Russian-Japanese War breaks out. Theodore Roosevelt wins presidential election.

1905—Treaty of Portsmouth signed, ending Russian-Japanese War.

1906—U.S. troops occupy Cuba.

1907—President Roosevelt bars all Japanese immigration. Oklahoma enters the Union.

1908—William Howard Taft becomes president. Grover Cleveland dies in Princeton, New Jersey. Lyndon B. Johnson is born near Stonewall, Texas.

1909—NAACP is founded under W.E.B. DuBois

1910—China abolishes slavery.

1911—Chinese Revolution begins. Ronald Reagan is born in Tampico, Illinois.

1912—Woodrow Wilson is elected president. Arizona and New Mexico become states.

1913—Federal income tax is introduced in U.S. through the Sixteenth Amendment. Richard Nixon is born in Yorba Linda, California. Gerald Ford is born in Omaha, Nebraska.

1914—World War I begins.

1915—British liner *Lusitania* is sunk by German submarine.

1916—Wilson is reelected president.

1917—U.S. breaks diplomatic relations with Germany. Czar Nicholas of Russia abdicates as revolution begins. U.S. declares war on Austria-Hungary. John F. Kennedy is born in Brookline, Massachusetts.

1918—Wilson proclaims "Fourteen Points" as war aims. On November 11, armistice is signed between Allies and Germany.

1919—Eighteenth Amendment prohibits sale and manufacture of intoxicating liquors. Wilson presides over first League of Nations; wins Nobel Peace Prize. Theodore Roosevelt dies in Oyster Bay, New York.

1920—Nineteenth Amendment (women's suffrage) is passed. Warren Harding is elected president.

1921—Adolf Hitler's stormtroopers begin to terrorize political opponents.

1922—Irish Free State is established. Soviet states form USSR. Benito Mussolini forms Fascist government in Italy.

1923—President Harding dies in San Francisco, California; he is succeeded by Vice-President Calvin Coolidge.

1924—Coolidge is elected president. Woodrow Wilson dies in Washington, D.C. James Carter is born in Plains, Georgia. George Bush is born in Milton, Massachusetts.

1925—Hitler reorganizes Nazi Party and publishes first volume of *Mein Kampf.*

1926—Fascist youth organizations founded in Germany and Italy. Republic of Lebanon proclaimed.

1927—Stalin becomes Soviet dictator. Economic conference in Geneva attended by fifty-two nations.

1928—Herbert Hoover is elected president. U.S. and many other nations sign Kellogg-Briand pacts to outlaw war.

1929—Stock prices in New York crash on "Black Thursday"; the Great Depression begins.

1930—Bank of U.S. and its many branches close (most significant bank failure of the year). William Howard Taft dies in Washington, D.C.

1931—Emigration from U.S. exceeds immigration for first time as Depression deepens.

1932—Franklin D. Roosevelt wins presidential election in a Democratic landslide.

1933—First concentration camps are erected in Germany. U.S. recognizes USSR and resumes trade. Twenty-First Amendment repeals prohibition. Calvin Coolidge dies in Northampton, Massachusetts.

1934—Severe dust storms hit Plains states. President Roosevelt passes U.S. Social Security Act.

1936—Roosevelt is reelected. Spanish Civil War begins. Hitler and Mussolini form Rome-Berlin Axis.

1937—Roosevelt signs Neutrality Act.

1938—Roosevelt sends appeal to Hitler and Mussolini to settle European problems amicably.

1939—Germany takes over Czechoslovakia and invades Poland, starting World War II.

1940—Roosevelt is reelected for a third term.

1941—Japan bombs Pearl Harbor, U.S. declares war on Japan. Germany and Italy declare war on U.S.; U.S. then declares war on them.

1942—Allies agree not to make separate peace treaties with the enemies. U.S. government transfers more than 100,000 Nisei (Japanese-Americans) from west coast to inland concentration camps.

1943—Allied bombings of Germany begin.

1944—Roosevelt is reelected for a fourth term. Allied forces invade Normandy on D-Day.

1945—President Franklin D. Roosevelt dies in Warm Springs, Georgia; Vice-President Harry S. Truman succeeds him. Mussolini is killed; Hitler commits suicide. Germany surrenders. U.S. drops atomic bomb on Hiroshima; Japan surrenders: end of World War II.

1946—U.N. General Assembly holds its first session in London. Peace conference of twenty-one nations is held in Paris.

1947—Peace treaties are signed in Paris. "Cold War" is in full swing.

1948—U.S. passes Marshall Plan Act, providing $17 billion in aid for Europe. U.S. recognizes new nation of Israel. India and Pakistan become free of British rule. Truman is elected president.

1949—Republic of Eire is proclaimed in Dublin. Russia blocks land route access from Western Germany to Berlin; airlift begins. U.S., France, and Britain agree to merge their zones of occupation in West Germany. Apartheid program begins in South Africa.

1950—Riots in Johannesburg, South Africa, against apartheid. North Korea invades South Korea. U.N. forces land in South Korea and recapture Seoul.

1951—Twenty-Second Amendment limits president to two terms.

1952—Dwight D. Eisenhower resigns as supreme commander in Europe and is elected president.

1953—Stalin dies; struggle for power in Russia follows. Rosenbergs are executed for espionage.

1954—U.S. and Japan sign mutual defense agreement.

1955—Blacks in Montgomery, Alabama, boycott segregated bus lines.

1956—Eisenhower is reelected president. Soviet troops march into Hungary.

1957—U.S. agrees to withdraw ground forces from Japan. Russia launches first satellite, *Sputnik*.

1958—European Common Market comes into being. Fidel Castro begins war against Batista government in Cuba.

1959—Alaska becomes the forty-ninth state. Hawaii becomes fiftieth state. Castro becomes premier of Cuba. De Gaulle is proclaimed president of the Fifth Republic of France.

1960—Historic debates between Senator John F. Kennedy and Vice-President Richard Nixon are televised. Kennedy is elected president. Brezhnev becomes president of USSR.

1961—Berlin Wall is constructed. Kennedy and Khrushchev confer in Vienna. In Bay of Pigs incident, Cubans trained by CIA attempt to overthrow Castro.

1962—U.S. military council is established in South Vietnam.

1963—Riots and beatings by police and whites mark civil rights demonstrations in Birmingham, Alabama; 30,000 troops are called out, Martin Luther King, Jr., is arrested. Freedom marchers descend on Washington, D.C., to demonstrate. President Kennedy is assassinated in Dallas, Texas; Vice-President Lyndon B. Johnson is sworn in as president.

1964—U.S. aircraft bomb North Vietnam. Johnson is elected president. Herbert Hoover dies in New York City.

1965—U.S. combat troops arrive in South Vietnam.

1966—Thousands protest U.S. policy in Vietnam. National Guard quells race riots in Chicago.

1967—Six-Day War between Israel and Arab nations.

1968—Martin Luther King, Jr., is assassinated in Memphis, Tennessee. Senator Robert Kennedy is assassinated in Los Angeles. Riots and police brutality take place at Democratic National Convention in Chicago. Richard Nixon is elected president. Czechoslovakia is invaded by Soviet troops.

1969—Dwight D. Eisenhower dies in Washington, D.C. Hundreds of thousands of people in several U.S. cities demonstrate against Vietnam War.

1970—Four Vietnam War protesters are killed by National Guardsmen at Kent State University in Ohio.

1971—Twenty-Sixth Amendment allows eighteen-year-olds to vote.

1972—Nixon visits Communist China; is reelected president in near-record landslide. Watergate affair begins when five men are arrested in the Watergate hotel complex in Washington, D.C. Nixon announces resignations of aides Haldeman, Ehrlichman, and Dean and Attorney General Kleindienst as a result of Watergate-related charges. Harry S. Truman dies in Kansas City, Missouri.

1973—Vice-President Spiro Agnew resigns; Gerald Ford is named vice-president. Vietnam peace treaty is formally approved after nineteen months of negotiations. Lyndon B. Johnson dies in San Antonio, Texas.

1974—As a result of Watergate cover-up, impeachment is considered; Nixon resigns and Ford becomes president. Ford pardons Nixon and grants limited amnesty to Vietnam War draft evaders and military deserters.

1975—U.S. civilians are evacuated from Saigon, South Vietnam, as Communist forces complete takeover of South Vietnam.

1976—U.S. celebrates its Bicentennial. James Earl Carter becomes president.

1977—Carter pardons most Vietnam draft evaders, numbering some 10,000.

1980—Ronald Reagan is elected president.

1981—President Reagan is shot in the chest in assassination attempt. Sandra Day O'Connor is appointed first woman justice of the Supreme Court.

1983—U.S. troops invade island of Grenada.

1984—Reagan is reelected president. Democratic candidate Walter Mondale's running mate, Geraldine Ferraro, is the first woman selected for vice-president by a major U.S. political party.

1985—Soviet Communist Party secretary Konstantin Chernenko dies; Mikhail Gorbachev succeeds him. U.S. and Soviet officials discuss arms control in Geneva. Reagan and Gorbachev hold summit conference in Geneva. Racial tensions accelerate in South Africa.

1986—Space shuttle *Challenger* explodes shortly after takeoff; crew of seven dies. U.S. bombs bases in Libya. Corazon Aquino defeats Ferdinand Marcos in Philippine presidential election.

1987—Iraqi missile rips the U.S. frigate *Stark* in the Persian Gulf, killing thirty-seven American sailors. Congress holds hearings to investigate sale of U.S. arms to Iran to finance Nicaraguan *contra* movement.

1988—President Reagan and Soviet leader Gorbachev sign INF treaty, eliminating intermediate nuclear forces. Severe drought sweeps the United States. George Bush is elected president.

1989—East Germany opens Berlin Wall, allowing citizens free exit. Communists lose control of governments in Poland, Romania, and Czechoslovakia. Chinese troops massacre over 1,000 pro-democracy student demonstrators in Beijing's Tiananmen Square.

1990—Iraq annexes Kuwait, provoking the threat of war. East and West Germany are reunited. The Cold War between the United States and the Soviet Union comes to a close. Several Soviet republics make moves toward independence.

1991—Backed by a coalition of members of the United Nations, U.S. troops drive Iraqis from Kuwait. Latvia, Lithuania, and Estonia withdraw from the USSR. The Soviet Union dissolves as its republics secede to form a Commonwealth of Independent States.

1992—U.N. forces fail to stop fighting in territories of former Yugoslavia. More than fifty people are killed and more than six hundred buildings burned in rioting in Los Angeles. U.S. unemployment reaches eight-year high. Hurricane Andrew devastates southern Florida and parts of Louisiana. International relief supplies and troops are sent to combat famine and violence in Somalia.

1993—U.S.-led forces use airplanes and missiles to attack military targets in Iraq. William Jefferson Clinton becomes the forty-second U.S. president.

1994—Richard M. Nixon dies in New York City.

Index

Page numbers in boldface type indicate illustrations.

About the Author

Susan Clinton holds a Ph.D. in English and is a part-time teacher of English Literature at Northwestern University in Chicago. Her articles have appeared in such publications as *Consumer's Digest*, *Family Style Magazine*, and the Chicago *Reader*. In addition, she has contributed biographical and historical articles to *Encyclopaedia Britannica* and *Compton's Encyclopedia*, and has written reader stories and other materials for a number of educational publishers. Ms. Clinton lives in Chicago with her husband, Pat, and their two boys.